# STANDARD OF EXCELLENCE

## COMPREHEN D METHOD

### By Bruce Pearson

Dear Student:

Congratulations! You have successfully attained the first level in achieving a standard of excellence in music-making. By now, you have discovered that careful study and regular practice have brought you the joy and satisfaction of making beautiful music.

You are now ready to move to the next level in your music-making. I want to welcome you to STANDARD OF EXCELLENCE Book 2. I also want to wish you continued success and enjoyment.

Best wishes,

*Bruce Pearson*

## Practicing - the key to EXCELLENCE!

▶ Make practicing part of your daily schedule. If you plan practicing as you do any other activity, you will find plenty of time for it.

▶ Try to practice in the same place every day. Choose a place where you can concentrate on making music. Start with a regular and familiar warm-up routine, including long tones and simple technical exercises. Like an athlete, you need to warm-up your mind and muscles before you begin performing.

▶ Set goals for every practice session. Keep track of your practice time and progress on the front cover Practice Journal.

▶ Practice the hard spots in your lesson assignment and band music over and over, until you can play them perfectly.

▶ Spend time practicing both alone and with the STANDARD OF EXCELLENCE recorded accompaniments.

▶ At the end of each practice session, play something fun.

ISBN 0-8497-5959-5

KJOS NEIL A. KJOS MUSIC COMPANY, PUBLISHER

W22XR

# REVIEW

## G MAJOR KEY SIGNATURE

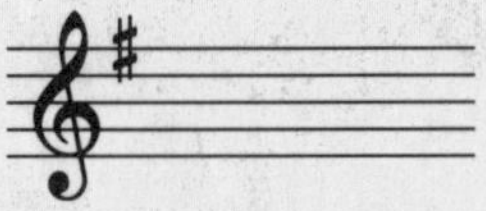

## 1 WARM-UP - Band Arrangement

**Andante**

f


## 2 G MAJOR SCALE SKILL (Concert B♭ Major)

**Moderato**

Arpeggio
Chords
mf

▶ Lines with a medal are *Achievement Lines.* The chart on page 47 can be used to record your progress.

## 3 BOTANY BAY

**Page 40**

Australian Folk Song

**Moderato**

mp
mf
f
mp


▶ When you see a page number followed by an arrow, *Excellerate* to the page indicated for additional studies.

## 4 DRIVE TIME

**Andante**

mp

## 5 SHEPHERD'S HEY

English Folk Song

**Moderato**

Fine
mf
D.C. al Fine
p

## REVIEW

## C MAJOR KEY SIGNATURE

**6** **C MAJOR SCALE SKILL (Concert E♭ Major)**

▶ Are you playing with a good embouchure and hand position?

**7** **MOLLY MALONE**

Irish Folk Song

**8** **NO LOOKING BACK** Page 40 ▶

**9** **TURKISH MARCH**

Wolfgang Amadeus Mozart (1756 - 1791)

**10** **HYMN OF THANKSGIVING - Band Arrangement**

Johann Crüger (1598 - 1662)
arr. Bruce Pearson (b. 1942)

## REVIEW

## D MAJOR
## KEY SIGNATURE

**11** **WARM-UP - Band Arrangement**

Andante

*mf*

**12** **D MAJOR SCALE SKILL (Concert F Major)**

Moderato

*f* , Arpeggio , Chords

**13** **KNUCKLEBUSTER**

Moderato

*mf*

1. , 2.

**14** **GIVE ME THAT OLD TIME RELIGION**

Page 40 ▶

American Spiritual

Allegro

*f*

clap

**15** _____ Composer _____

your name

Moderato

▶ Compose an ending for this melody. Title and play your composition.

**16** **FOR BARITONE SAXOPHONES ONLY**

Page 40 ▶

Moderato

C

alternate

*mf*

▶ *Use the alternate C fingering when moving from B to C or C to B.

| SYNCOPATION |  | A rhythmic effect which places emphasis on a weak or unaccented part of the measure. |
|---|---|---|
| INTERVAL |  | The distance between any two notes. |

## 17 SYNCOPATION SENSATION

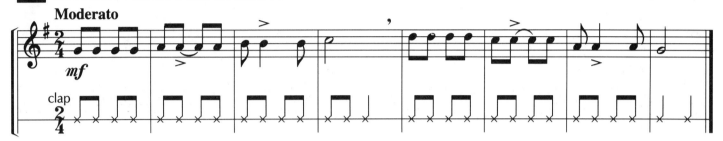

## 18 THE RIDDLE SONG

American Folk Song

▶ Write in the counting and clap the rhythm before you play.

## 19 NOBODY KNOWS THE TROUBLE I'VE SEEN

American Spiritual

## 20 INTERVAL INQUIRY

▶ Sing this exercise using the numbers before you play.

## 21 GO FOR EXCELLENCE!

American Folk Song

W22XR

| E MINOR KEY SIGNATURE | TEMPO<br><br>*Accelerando (accel.)* | DIVISI<br><br>UNISON | Part of the section plays the top notes and part of the section plays the bottom notes.<br><br>Everyone plays the same notes. |
|---|---|---|---|
| **E minor** has the same key signature as **G major**. | Gradually increase the tempo. | | |

**22  WARM-UP - Band Arrangement**

Andante

**23  E NATURAL MINOR SCALE SKILL (Concert G Natural Minor)**

Moderato

**24  E HARMONIC MINOR SCALE SKILL (Concert G Harmonic Minor)**

Moderato

**25  MINKA, MINKA**

Moderato

Ukrainian Folk Song

2nd time - *accel.*

*Hey!*

**26  LAREDO - Duet**

Moderato

Mexican Folk Song

▶ Name the interval between the top and bottom notes of the last measure. _____

**27  TURNING YOU LOOSE**

Moderato

**28  FOR BARITONE SAXOPHONES ONLY**

Andante

## DAL SEGNO AL FINE (D.S. AL FINE)

Go back to the sign (𝄋) and play until the *Fine.*

# JOYEUX NOËL
**Band Arrangement**

French Carol
arr. Chuck Elledge (b. 1961)

## 29 GO FOR EXCELLENCE!

W22XR

| F MAJOR KEY SIGNATURE | 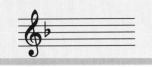 | This key signature means play all B's as B flats. |
| --- | --- | --- |

| TEXTURES | **Monophony** - a single unaccompanied melody.<br>**Polyphony** - two or more melodies played at the same time. |
| --- | --- |

### 36 F MAJOR SCALE SKILL (Concert A♭ Major)

### 37 GREASED LIGHTNING

### 38 PARTNER SONGS - Duet

Traditional

▶ For an example of monophony, play line A or line B alone. For an example of polyphony, play line A while someone else plays line B.

### 39 GO FOR EXCELLENCE!

Stephen Foster (1826 - 1864)

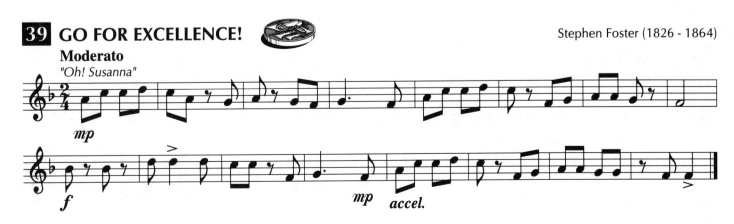

## ENHARMONICS

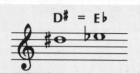

D# = Eb

Notes that sound the same but are written differently.

## ARTICULATION

*Staccato* (dot placed above or below note) - Play short and detached.

## TEMPO

**Allegretto -**
light and lively; slightly slower than **Allegro.**

**40 WARM-UP - Band Arrangement**

Andante

mf

▶ *Use the alternate F# fingering.

**41 CHROMATIC CAPERS**

Moderato

Eb

f

enharmonic

enharmonic

**42 SHENANDOAH**

American Folk Song

Andante

mp

**43 THEME FROM SYMPHONY NO. 94**

Franz Joseph Haydn (1732 - 1809)

Andante

p

**44 PARADE OF THE TIN SOLDIERS**

Léon Jessel (1871 - 1942)

Allegretto

mf

1.

2.

**45 FOR BARITONE SAXOPHONES ONLY**

Page 40 ▌▌▌▶

Allegro

mf

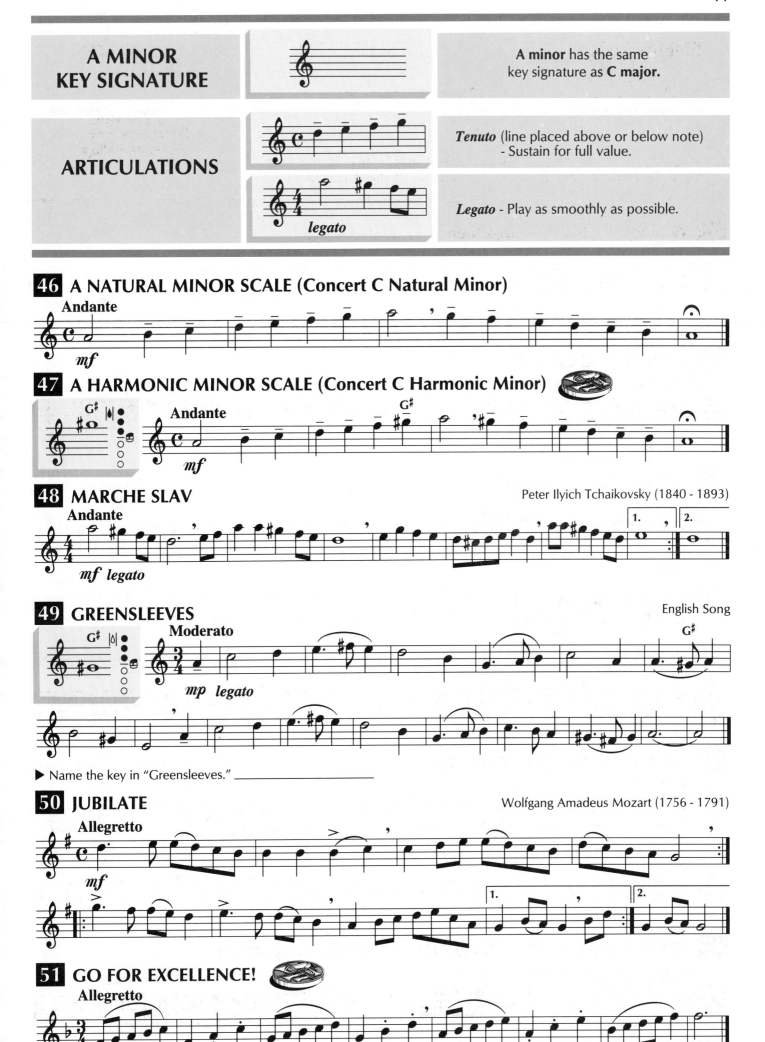

**A MINOR KEY SIGNATURE**

A **minor** has the same key signature as **C major.**

**ARTICULATIONS**

*Tenuto* (line placed above or below note) - Sustain for full value.

*legato*

*Legato* - Play as smoothly as possible.

**46 A NATURAL MINOR SCALE (Concert C Natural Minor)**

Andante

*mf*

**47 A HARMONIC MINOR SCALE (Concert C Harmonic Minor)**

Andante

*mf*

**48 MARCHE SLAV**

Peter Ilyich Tchaikovsky (1840 - 1893)

Andante

*mf legato*

1.    2.

**49 GREENSLEEVES**

English Song

Moderato

*mp legato*

▶ Name the key in "Greensleeves." _____

**50 JUBILATE**

Wolfgang Amadeus Mozart (1756 - 1791)

Allegretto

*mf*

1.    2.

**51 GO FOR EXCELLENCE!**

Allegretto

*mf*

W22XR

## TEXTURE

**Melody and Accompaniment** - main melody is accompanied by chords or less important melodies called **countermelodies**.

**52 WARM-UP**

**53 HABAÑERA** — Georges Bizet (1838 - 1875)

▶ *Use the alternate F♯ fingering.

**54 SMOOTH AS SILK**

**55 HEY HO - Round (Canon)** — Medieval Song

**56 THE BRITISH GRENADIERS - Duet** — English Folk Song

A. Melody

B. Countermelody

**57 FOR BARITONE SAXOPHONES ONLY**

 **ENHARMONICS**

**CHORD**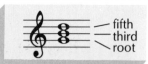

Two or more pitches sounded at the same time.

## 63 WARM-UP - Band Arrangement

**Andante**

## 64 DANISH ROLL

Danish Folk Song

**Moderato**

## 65 RUSSIAN SAILORS' DANCE

Reinhold Glière (1875 - 1956)

**Allegretto**

## 66 CHORD CAPERS

▶ Listen for the different types of chords played by the full band.

## 67 FOR BARITONE SAXOPHONES ONLY

Page 41 ▶

▶ *Use the alternate B♭ fingerings.

W22XR

## ENHARMONICS

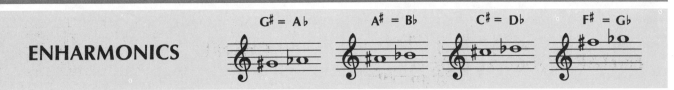

G♯ = A♭    A♯ = B♭    C♯ = D♭    F♯ = G♭

**68 CHROMATIC SCALE SKILL**

Andante

▶ *Use the alternate F♯/G♭ fingering.

**69 SAILING THE HIGH SEAS**

Moderato

**70 CHROMATIC MARCH**

Allegro

𝆏 - 1st time
𝆑 - 2nd time

▶ *Use the alternate F♯/G♭ fingering.

**71 MANHATTAN BEACH MARCH**

John Philip Sousa (1854 - 1932)

Allegro

**72 GO FOR EXCELLENCE!**

Moderato

▶ Play using each of the following articulations:    A.    B.    C.    D.

## DA CAPO AL CODA (D.C. AL CODA)

Go back to the beginning and play until the coda sign (⊕). When you reach the coda sign, skip to the *Coda* (⊕).

## ROCK ISLAND EXPRESS
**Band Arrangement**

Chuck Elledge (b. 1961)

## TIME SIGNATURE

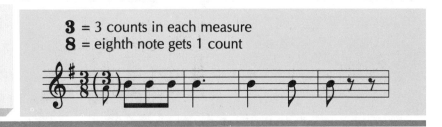

**3** = 3 counts in each measure
**8** = eighth note gets 1 count

### 73 FINLANDIA - Band Arrangement

Jean Sibelius (1865 - 1957)
arr. Bruce Pearson (b. 1942)

**Moderato**

Permission granted for sale outside of the U.S.A. by Breitkopf & Härtel.
© Breitkopf & Härtel, Wiesbaden, Germany

### 74 TRIPLE PLAY

**Allegretto**

▶ Write in the counting and clap the rhythm before you play.

### 75 WE THREE KINGS

John H. Hopkins, Jr. (1820 - 1891)

**Andante**

▶ Name the key in "We Three Kings." _____

### 76 GO FOR EXCELLENCE!

**Allegro**

## A MAJOR KEY SIGNATURE

This key signature means play all F's as F sharps, all C's as C sharps, and all G's as G sharps.

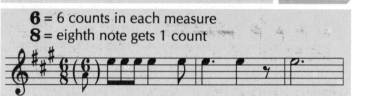

## TIME SIGNATURE

**6** = 6 counts in each measure
**8** = eighth note gets 1 count

**77 A MAJOR SCALE SKILL (Concert C Major)**

Andante · Arpeggio · Chords · mf

**78 OVER THE RIVER**

Allegro · f · Traditional · 1. · 2.

▶ Draw in a breath mark at the end of each phrase.

**79 OODLES OF NOODLES**

Moderato · mf

**80 UPS AND DOWNS**

Allegretto · mp

▶ Write in the counting and draw in the bar lines before you play.

**81 FOR BARITONE SAXOPHONES ONLY**

 Page 41 ▶

alternate · alternate · A Moderato · mf · B

▶ * Use the alternate B♭ fingerings.

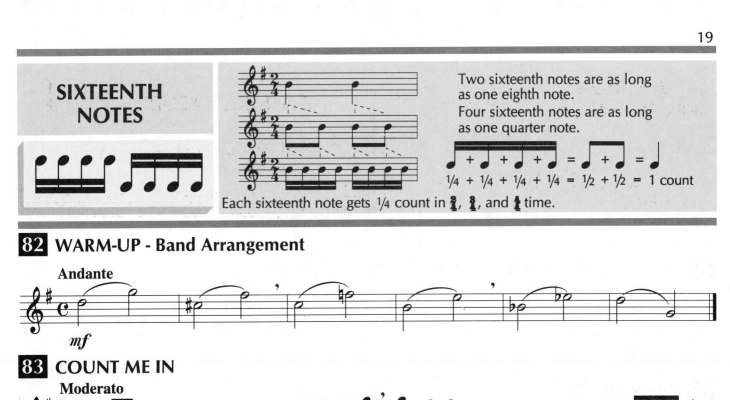

## SIXTEENTH NOTES

Two sixteenth notes are as long as one eighth note.
Four sixteenth notes are as long as one quarter note.

¼ + ¼ + ¼ + ¼ = ½ + ½ = 1 count

Each sixteenth note gets ¼ count in ²⁄₂, ²⁄₄, and ²⁄₈ time.

**82 WARM-UP - Band Arrangement**

Andante

mf

**83 COUNT ME IN**

Moderato

mf

▶ Write in the counting and clap the rhythm before you play.

**84 KEMO KIMO**

American Folk Song

Allegretto

p     f     p     f

p     f

**85 FRENCH MARCHING SONG**

French Folk Song

Allegro

1.     2.

f

▶ Name the interval between the first and second notes. _____

**86 FENG YANG SONG**

Chinese Folk Song

Moderato

mp

**87 GO FOR EXCELLENCE!**

Patrick Gilmore (1829 - 1892)

Allegro

"When Johnny Comes Marching Home"

mp     mf

f     mp

W22XR

20

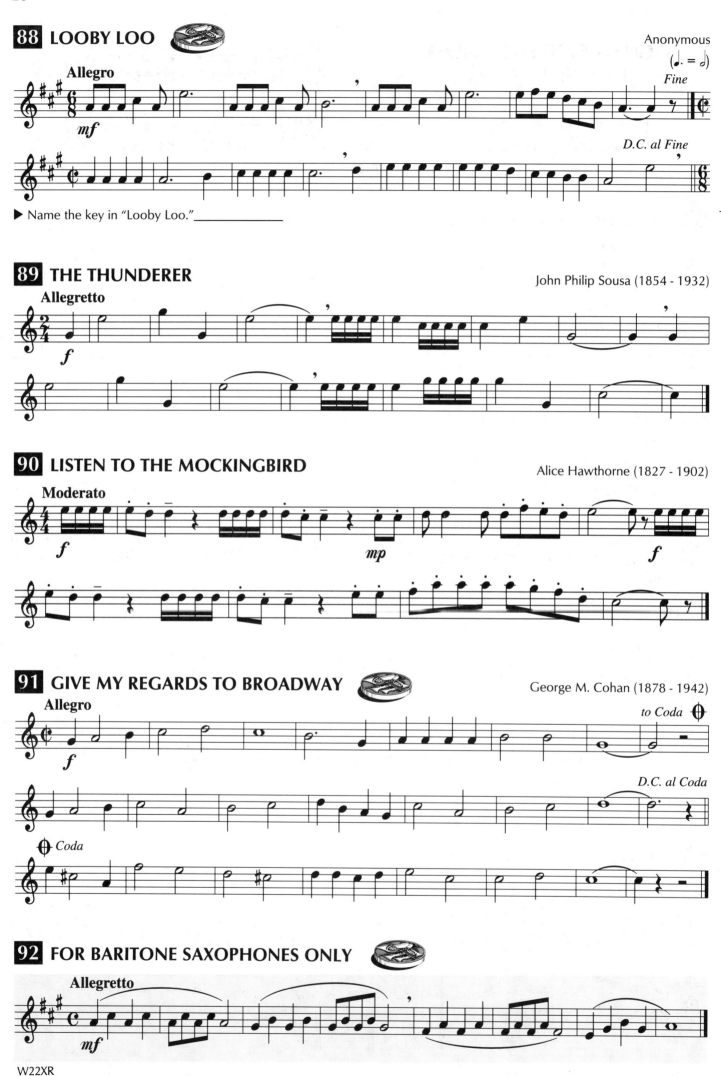

**88 LOOBY LOO**

Anonymous

▶ Name the key in "Looby Loo." _____

**89 THE THUNDERER**

John Philip Sousa (1854 - 1932)

**90 LISTEN TO THE MOCKINGBIRD**

Alice Hawthorne (1827 - 1902)

**91 GIVE MY REGARDS TO BROADWAY**

George M. Cohan (1878 - 1942)

**92 FOR BARITONE SAXOPHONES ONLY**

## EIGHTH/SIXTEENTH NOTE COMBINATIONS

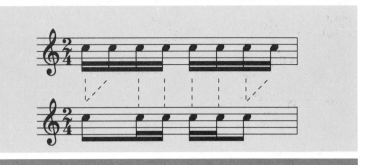

**93 CHESTER - Band Arrangement**

William Billings (1746 - 1800)
arr. Bruce Pearson (b. 1942)

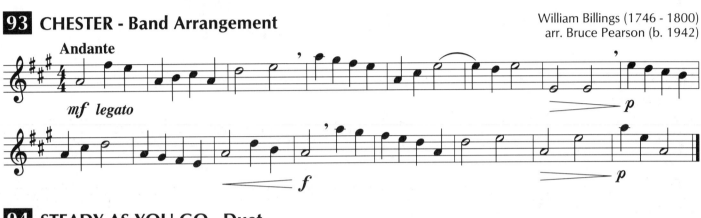

**94 STEADY AS YOU GO - Duet**

**95 TIRRA LIRRA LOO**

Canadian Folk Song

▶ Write in the counting and clap the rhythm before you play.

**96 GO FOR EXCELLENCE!**

American Folk Song

W22XR

# TURKISH MARCH
## from "The Ruins of Athens"
### Solo with Piano Accompaniment

Ludwig van Beethoven (1770 - 1827)
arr. Bruce Pearson (b. 1942)

24

## 97 BLAZIN'

▶ Name the interval between the first and second notes. _____
▶ *Use the alternate C fingering.

## 98 AMERICAN PATROL
Frank W. Meacham (1856 - 1909)

## 99 KERRY DANCE
Irish Folk Song

## 100 GAVOTTE
Page 41
James Hook (1746 - 1827)

## 101 FOR BARITONE SAXOPHONES ONLY

 **SINGLE SIXTEENTH NOTE**

A single sixteenth note is half as long as an eighth note.

♪ = ¼ count in 𝄴, 𝄵, and 𝄵 time.

**DOTTED EIGHTH NOTE**

A dot after a note adds half the value of the note.

♪ + · = ♪ + ♪ = ♪·

**DOTTED EIGHTH/ SIXTEENTH NOTE COMBINATION**

**102 DOTS OF FUN**

Moderato

**103 LITTLE BROWN JUG - Duet**

Joseph Eastburn Winner (1837 - 1918)

Allegro

▶ Write in the counting and clap the rhythm before you play.

**104 OUR BOYS WILL SHINE TONIGHT**

College Song

Allegretto

▶ Draw in a breath mark at the end of each phrase.

**105** _____ Composer _____

your name

▶ Compose an ending for this melody. Be sure to use the ♪· rhythm. Title and play your composition.

**106 GO FOR EXCELLENCE!**

Georges Bizet (1838 - 1875)

Allegro
"Farandole from L'Arlesienne Suite"

W22XR

**107** **CUCKOO SONG**

Austrian Folk Song

Andante

**108** **MARCH MILITAIRE** Page 41

Franz Schubert (1797 - 1828)

Allegretto

*to Coda*

*D.C. al Coda*

*Coda*

**109** **ST. ANTHONY CHORALE**

Franz Joseph Haydn (1732 - 1809)

Andante

*Fine*

*D.C. al Fine*

**110** _____ Composer _____

your name

a.     b.     c.     d.

▶ Arrange these melodic pieces in any order to build a tune you like. You may use pieces more than once. Title and play your composition.

**111** **FOR BARITONE SAXOPHONES ONLY**

Allegro

**EIGHTH NOTE TRIPLET**

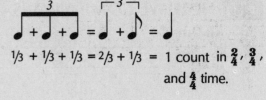

$\frac{1}{3} + \frac{1}{3} + \frac{1}{3} = \frac{2}{3} + \frac{1}{3} = 1$ count in $\frac{2}{4}$, $\frac{3}{4}$, and $\frac{4}{4}$ time.

**TEMPO**

**Maestoso** - majestically

**112 TRIPLE TREAT**

**113 STARS OF THE HEAVENS - Duet** Page 41 Mexican Folk Song

**114 LIGHT CAVALRY OVERTURE** Franz von Suppé (1819 - 1895)

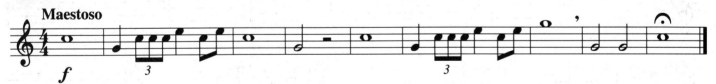

**115 GO FOR EXCELLENCE!**  Charles Gounod (1818 - 1893)

"Soldiers' Chorus from Faust"

W22XR

**116 HERE WE COME A-WASSAILING** — English Folk Song

**117 THEME FROM "ZAMPA"** — Ferdinand Herold (1791 - 1833)

**118 GO FOR EXCELLENCE!** — Peter Ilyich Tchaikovsky (1840 - 1893)

# CABO RICO
**Band Arrangement**

Chuck Elledge (b. 1961)

# RUDIMENTAL REGIMENT

**Band Arrangement**

Bruce Pearson (b. 1942)
and Chuck Elledge (b. 1961)

W22XR

# SUMMER'S RAIN
### Band Arrangement

Chuck Elledge (b. 1961)

# FRENCH MARKET BUZZARDS MARCH

**Band Arrangement**

Liberato Gallo
arr. Wendy Barden (b. 1955)

W22XR

# ROMANZA

**Ensemble**

Ludwig van Beethoven, Op. 40 (1770 - 1827)
arr. Janice Strobl Kersey (b. 1959)

# HORNPIPE from "Water Music"

**Ensemble**

George Frideric Handel (1685 - 1759)
arr. Janice Strobl Kersey (b. 1959)

W22XR

# MINUET AND ALLEGRO
## Solo with Piano Accompaniment

## Minuet

Wolfgang Amadeus Mozart (1756 - 1791)
arr. Bruce Pearson (b. 1942)

## Allegro

# EXCELLERATORS - FOR BARITONE SAXOPHONES ONLY

▶ *Use the alternate C fingering.

# EXCELLERATORS - FOR BARITONE SAXOPHONES ONLY

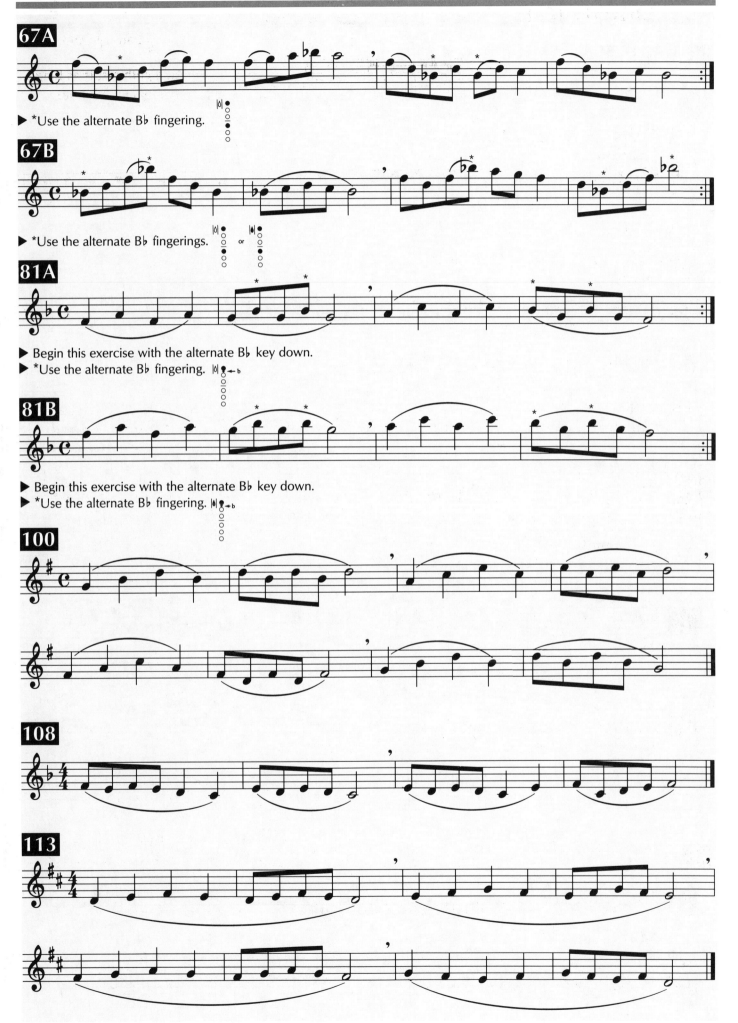

**67A**

▶ *Use the alternate B♭ fingering.

**67B**

▶ *Use the alternate B♭ fingerings.

**81A**

▶ Begin this exercise with the alternate B♭ key down.
▶ *Use the alternate B♭ fingering.

**81B**

▶ Begin this exercise with the alternate B♭ key down.
▶ *Use the alternate B♭ fingering.

**100**

**108**

**113**

# SCALE STUDIES

### G MAJOR SCALE SKILL (Concert B♭ Major)

### E HARMONIC MINOR SCALE (Concert G Harmonic Minor)

### C MAJOR SCALE (Concert E♭ Major)

### A HARMONIC MINOR SCALE (Concert C Harmonic Minor)

# SCALE STUDIES

## D MAJOR SCALE (Concert F Major)

## F MAJOR SCALE (Concert Ab Major)

## A MAJOR SCALE (Concert C Major)

## CHROMATIC SCALE

# RHYTHM STUDIES

# RHYTHM STUDIES

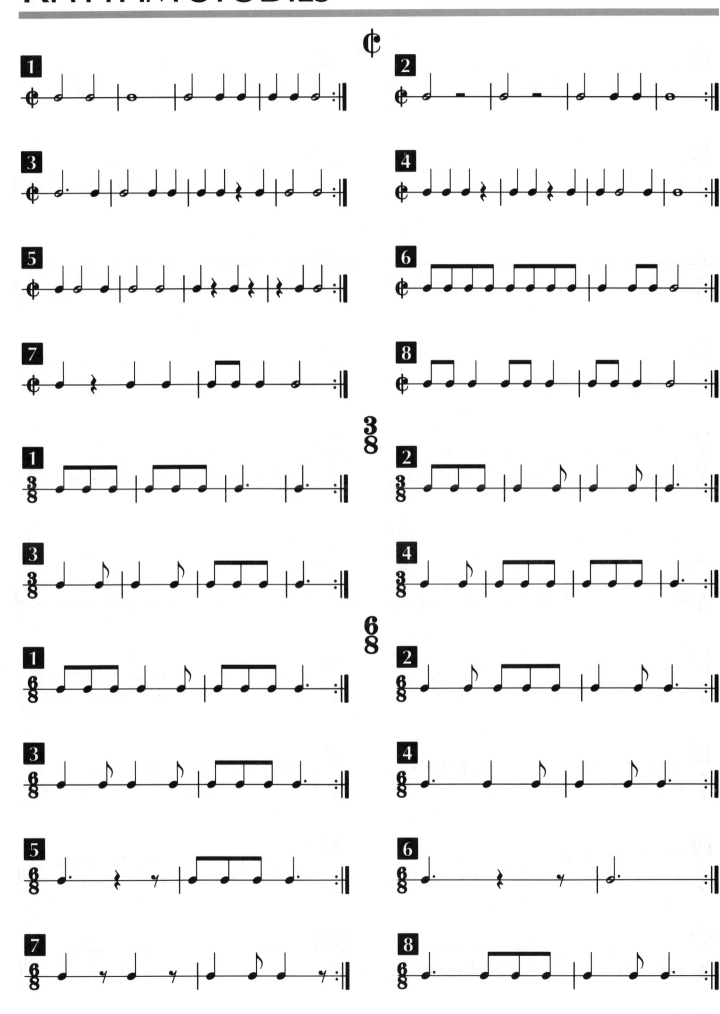

# GLOSSARY/INDEX

# STANDARD OF EXCELLENCE

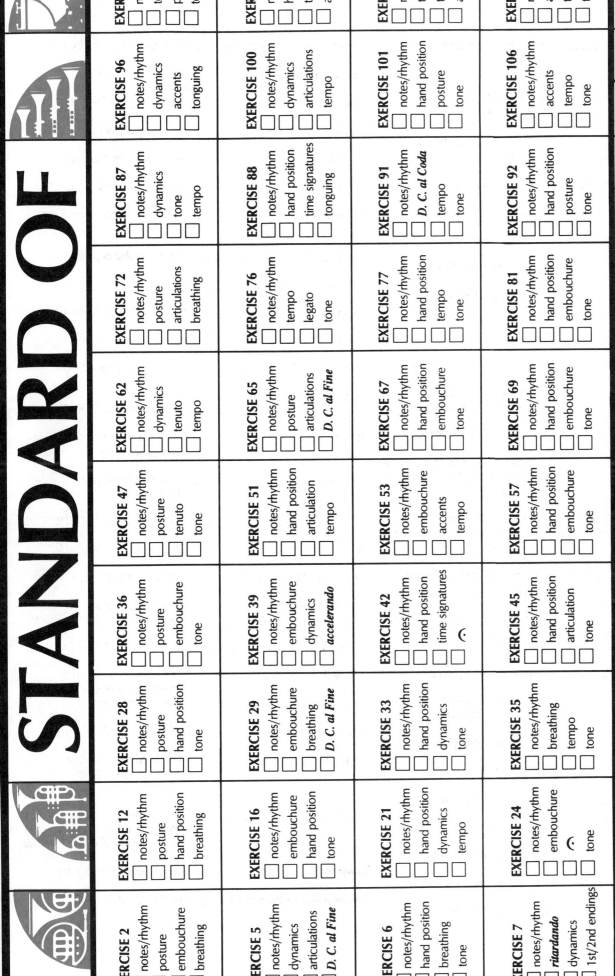

**EXERCISE 2**
- [ ] notes/rhythm
- [ ] posture
- [ ] embouchure
- [ ] breathing

**EXERCISE 5**
- [ ] notes/rhythm
- [ ] dynamics
- [ ] articulations
- [ ] *D. C. al Fine*

**EXERCISE 6**
- [ ] notes/rhythm
- [ ] hand position
- [ ] breathing
- [ ] tone

**EXERCISE 7**
- [ ] notes/rhythm
- [ ] *ritardando*
- [ ] dynamics
- [ ] 1st/2nd endings

**EXERCISE 12**
- [ ] notes/rhythm
- [ ] posture
- [ ] hand position
- [ ] breathing

**EXERCISE 16**
- [ ] notes/rhythm
- [ ] embouchure
- [ ] hand position
- [ ] tone

**EXERCISE 21**
- [ ] notes/rhythm
- [ ] hand position
- [ ] dynamics
- [ ] tempo

**EXERCISE 24**
- [ ] notes/rhythm
- [ ] embouchure
- [ ] 𝄐
- [ ] tone

**EXERCISE 28**
- [ ] notes/rhythm
- [ ] posture
- [ ] hand position
- [ ] tone

**EXERCISE 29**
- [ ] notes/rhythm
- [ ] embouchure
- [ ] breathing
- [ ] *D. C. al Fine*

**EXERCISE 33**
- [ ] notes/rhythm
- [ ] hand position
- [ ] dynamics
- [ ] tone

**EXERCISE 35**
- [ ] notes/rhythm
- [ ] breathing
- [ ] tempo
- [ ] tone

**EXERCISE 36**
- [ ] notes/rhythm
- [ ] posture
- [ ] embouchure
- [ ] tone

**EXERCISE 39**
- [ ] notes/rhythm
- [ ] embouchure
- [ ] dynamics
- [ ] *accelerando*

**EXERCISE 42**
- [ ] notes/rhythm
- [ ] hand position
- [ ] time signatures
- [ ] 𝄐

**EXERCISE 45**
- [ ] notes/rhythm
- [ ] hand position
- [ ] articulation
- [ ] tone

**EXERCISE 47**
- [ ] notes/rhythm
- [ ] posture
- [ ] tenuto
- [ ] tone

**EXERCISE 51**
- [ ] notes/rhythm
- [ ] hand position
- [ ] articulation
- [ ] tempo

**EXERCISE 53**
- [ ] notes/rhythm
- [ ] embouchure
- [ ] accents
- [ ] tempo

**EXERCISE 57**
- [ ] notes/rhythm
- [ ] hand position
- [ ] embouchure
- [ ] tone

**EXERCISE 62**
- [ ] notes/rhythm
- [ ] dynamics
- [ ] tenuto
- [ ] tempo

**EXERCISE 65**
- [ ] notes/rhythm
- [ ] posture
- [ ] articulations
- [ ] *D. C. al Fine*

**EXERCISE 67**
- [ ] notes/rhythm
- [ ] hand position
- [ ] tempo
- [ ] tone

**EXERCISE 69**
- [ ] notes/rhythm
- [ ] hand position
- [ ] embouchure
- [ ] tone

**EXERCISE 72**
- [ ] notes/rhythm
- [ ] posture
- [ ] articulations
- [ ] breathing

**EXERCISE 76**
- [ ] notes/rhythm
- [ ] tempo
- [ ] legato
- [ ] tone

**EXERCISE 77**
- [ ] notes/rhythm
- [ ] hand position
- [ ] tempo
- [ ] tone

**EXERCISE 81**
- [ ] notes/rhythm
- [ ] hand position
- [ ] embouchure
- [ ] tone

**EXERCISE 87**
- [ ] notes/rhythm
- [ ] dynamics
- [ ] tone
- [ ] tempo

**EXERCISE 88**
- [ ] notes/rhythm
- [ ] hand position
- [ ] time signatures
- [ ] tonguing

**EXERCISE 91**
- [ ] notes/rhythm
- [ ] *D. C. al Coda*
- [ ] tempo
- [ ] tone

**EXERCISE 92**
- [ ] notes/rhythm
- [ ] hand position
- [ ] posture
- [ ] tone

**EXERCISE 96**
- [ ] notes/rhythm
- [ ] dynamics
- [ ] accents
- [ ] tonguing

**EXERCISE 100**
- [ ] notes/rhythm
- [ ] dynamics
- [ ] articulations
- [ ] tempo

**EXERCISE 101**
- [ ] notes/rhythm
- [ ] hand position
- [ ] posture
- [ ] tone

**EXERCISE 106**
- [ ] notes/rhythm
- [ ] accents
- [ ] tempo
- [ ] tone

**EXERCISE 111**
- [ ] notes/rhythm
- [ ] tempo
- [ ] posture
- [ ] tone

**EXERCISE 115**
- [ ] notes/rhythm
- [ ] hand position
- [ ] tempo
- [ ] accents

**EXERCISE 116**
- [ ] notes/rhythm
- [ ] time signatures
- [ ] tempo
- [ ] articulations

**EXERCISE 118**
- [ ] notes/rhythm
- [ ] articulations
- [ ] tempo
- [ ] tone

# THE E♭ BARITONE SAXOPHONE

## BARITONE SAXOPHONE CHECKLIST

☐ Sitting up straight

☐ Saxophone positioned on right side of body

☐ Neck strap properly adjusted

☐ Left and right thumbs correctly placed

☐ Head erect

☐ Fingers gently curved

☐ Wrists straight

☐ Elbows away from body

☐ Mouthpiece proper distance in mouth

☐ Top teeth resting directly on mouthpiece

☐ Equal pressure on all sides of mouthpiece

☐ Chin flat and pointed

☐ Breathing correctly by inhaling through corners of mouth

☐ Good tone produced

## BARITONE SAXOPHONE SURVIVAL KIT

☐ swab
☐ neck strap
☐ reed holder
☐ pencil
☐ band music

☐ soft, clean cloth
☐ extra reeds
☐ cork grease
☐ method book
☐ music stand